Test	Title	Page
Test 1	Add and subtract hundreds	2
Test 2	Place value	3
Test 3	Days	4
Test 4	1s, 10s, 100s and 1000s	5
Test 5	Fractions and decimals	6
Test 6	Adding several numbers	7
Test 7	Decimals – money and measuring	8
Test 8	Multiply and divide by 10	9
Test 9	Missing numbers	10
Test 10	Shapes	11
Test 11	Estimating	12
Test 12	Rounding up and down	13
Test 13	Negative numbers	14
Test 14	Days in the months	15
Test 15	Sequences	16
Test 16	Multiples	17
Test 17	Fractions	18
Test 18	Money	19
Test 19	Addition and subtraction	20
Test 20	Doubles and halves	21
Test 21	Remainders	22
Test 22	Angles	23
Test 23	Adding 3 numbers	24
Test 24	How long?	25
Test 25	Multiplication and division	26
Test 26	Money problems	27
Test 27	Which sign?	28
Test 28	Perimeters	29
Test 29	Measuring problems	30
Test 30	Mixed bag	31
Keep your score!		32

Test 1 Add and subtract hundreds

Complete these questions. Write your answers in the spaces. Try them all, then check your answers with the number-spotter.

90 + 14 = _____

112 − 12 = _____

450 + 17 = _____

600 − 8 = _____

257 + 7 = _____

704 − 9 = _____

300 + 126 = _____

826 − 326 = _____

131 + _____ = 200

500 − _____ = 493

_____ + 30 = 657

_____ − 13 = 790

156 + 70 = _____

604 − 585 = _____

382 + _____ = 490

495 − _____ = 250

Test 2 Place value

Answer each set of questions below. Write your answers in the spaces. Then check them with your number-spotter.

Fill in the spaces below to complete the sums.

2743 = 2000 + 700 + 40 + _____

6259 = 6000 + _____ + 50 + 9

1672 = _____ + 600 + 70 + 2

3364 = 3000 + 300 + _____ + 4

Write the following amounts in figures.

seven thousand, one hundred and forty-five _____

four thousand, eight hundred and sixty-two _____

five thousand, three hundred and twenty _____

Answer the following questions in words.

What is the figure 3 worth in the number 9321?

What is the figure 7 worth in the number 4876? _____

What is the figure 2 worth in the number 2155? _____

Test 3 Days

If today is Wednesday the 10th, work out the following dates. Write your answers in the spaces and check them with your number-spotter.

next Friday _____

last Monday _____

next Wednesday _____

last Wednesday _____

next Sunday _____

last Saturday _____

next Tuesday _____

last Thursday _____

What day was the 7th? _____

What day will the 15th be? _____

Test 4 1s, 10s, 100s, 1000s

Work out the answers to the following questions. Write your answers in the spaces. Then check them with your number-spotter.

What is…

1 more than 897? 898

1 less than 734? 733

10 more than 192? 202

10 less than 305? 295

100 more than 673? 773

100 less than 571? 471

1000 more than 226? 1226

1000 less than 4628? 3628

10 more than 1763? 1773

10 less than 6424? 6414

100 more than 3506? _____

100 less than 7961? _____

1000 more than 5740? _____

1000 less than 6002? _____

100 more than 2915? _____

100 less than 8057? _____

Test 5 Fractions and decimals

Write these fractions in their simplest terms. Check your answers with your number-spotter. The first one has been done for you.

$\frac{2}{8}$ is equal to $\frac{1}{4}$

$\frac{5}{10}$ is equal to _____

$\frac{2}{10}$ is equal to _____

$\frac{6}{8}$ is equal to _____

$\frac{4}{6}$ is equal to _____

$\frac{4}{8}$ is equal to _____

$\frac{2}{4}$ is equal to _____

$\frac{2}{6}$ is equal to _____

Circle the amounts that are…

greater than $\frac{1}{2}$ $\frac{4}{5}$ $\frac{1}{3}$ $\frac{3}{10}$ $\frac{5}{8}$

less than $\frac{1}{2}$ $\frac{2}{3}$ $\frac{3}{4}$ $\frac{3}{8}$ $\frac{1}{5}$

equivalent to $\frac{1}{2}$ $\frac{3}{5}$ 0.5 $\frac{2}{4}$ $\frac{7}{8}$

equivalent to $\frac{1}{4}$ 0.75 $\frac{2}{8}$ $\frac{7}{10}$ 0.25

Test 6 Adding several numbers

Work out the answers to the following sums. Write the answers in the spaces. Then check them with your number-spotter.

17 + 9 + 2 + 5 = _____

4 + 8 + 6 + 11 = _____

5 + 11 + 7 + 3 = _____

6 + 7 + 8 + 10 = _____

_____ + 4 + 9 + 6 = 24

12 + _____ + 7 + 2 = 30

20 + 40 + 60 = _____

30 + 70 + 50 = _____

15 + 7 + _____ + 6 = 33

19 + _____ + 11 + 2 = 39

80 + 30 + _____ = 180

_____ + 40 + 90 = 200

25 + _____ + 10 + 7 = 47

20 + 17 + _____ + 6 = 50

21 + 15 + _____ + 4 = 45

12 + _____ + 18 + 1 = 39

Test 7 Decimals – money and measuring

Decide which of the options in each list is the correct answer and put a ring around it. Then check your answers with the number-spotter.

most	99p	£1.01	£1.97	£9.90
longest	0.5m	3.5m	35m	5.3m
heaviest	4.5kg	45kg	5.4kg	54kg
most	5.0ml	50ml	0.5ml	5.5ml
shortest	2.2km	22km	0.2km	220km
lightest	7.3g	3.7g	73g	37g
least	£5.40	54p	530p	£3.50

Test 8 Multiply and divide by 10

Fill in the spaces to complete the sums. Check your answers with the number-spotter.

36 x 10 = _____

_____ x 10 = 720

250 ÷ 10 = _____

_____ ÷ 10 = 410

114 x 10 = _____

6000 ÷ 10 = _____

_____ x 10 = 5460

_____ ÷ 10 = 75

How many £1 coins are there in £20? _____

How many 10p coins are there in £15? _____

How much does a pack of 10 pencils cost when each pencil is 25p? _____

How much do 10 packs of pencils cost? _____

What is the cost of one book if a pack of 10 books is £4.50? _____

What is the cost of 10 books if 100 cost £72? _____

Test 9 Missing numbers

Work out which number should go in each of the spaces.
Write them in. Then check your answers with the number-spotter.

220 225 _____ 235 _____

570 _____ 550 _____ 530

875 _____ 855 845 _____

380 390 _____ _____ 420

1453 1454 _____ _____ 1457 _____ 1459

2781 2782 _____ _____ 2785 _____ 2787

3110 3120 _____ _____ 3150 _____ 3170

5870 _____ 5850 _____ 5830 _____ 5810

1670 1675 _____ _____ 1690 1695 _____

4235 _____ 4233 _____ 4231 4230 _____

Test 10 Shapes

Work out how many sides each of these shapes has, and add each row together. Write the totals in the spaces. Then check your answers with the number-spotter.

square	pentagon	triangle	_____
hexagon	triangle	oblong	_____
pentagon	hexagon	triangle	_____
triangle	octagon	square	_____
oblong	hexagon	square	_____
hexagon	octagon	triangle	_____
square	octagon	pentagon	_____
hexagon	triangle	pentagon	_____

Test 11 Estimating

Estimate the answers to the questions below. Write your answers in the spaces. Then use the number-spotter to see how close your estimates were.

This jug holds 1 litre when full.

Estimate how much is left in the jug. _____

This box of washing powder holds 2kg of washing powder when full.

Estimate how much powder is left in the box. _____

Which line is longer, line A or line B? _____

A

B

Which number do you think the arrow is pointing to on these lines?

0 ⬇ 50 _____

0 ⬇ 100 _____

20 ⬇ 80 _____

Test 12 Rounding up and down

Round these numbers up or down. Write your answers in the spaces. Then check your answers with the number-spotter.

Round these numbers to the nearest 10.

523 _____
247 _____
764 _____
386 _____

Round these numbers to the nearest 100.

441 _____
865 _____
173 _____
634 _____

Round these times to the nearest hour.

1.42 _____
5.20 _____
10.53 _____
7.12 _____

Round these distances to the nearest 10km.

54km _____
204km _____
547km _____
896km _____

Test 13 Negative numbers

Fill the blanks to complete each sequence. Check your answers with the number-spotter.

4 ___ 2 1 ___ –1 ___ –3 –4

–7 –6 ___ –4 –3 –2 –1 ___ 1

–10 –8 –6 ___ –2 ___ 2

50 40 30 ___ 10 0 –10 ___ –30

Circle the lowest temperature.

3°C   –7°C   –1°C   1°C   –4°C   –3°C

12°C   5°C   30°C   –2°C   –12°C   25°C

6°C   –21°C   20°C   12°C   –6°C   –3°C

Circle the highest temperature.

–8°C   2°C   –5°C   –2°C   0°C   –6°C

–5°C   5°C   15°C   –20°C   10°C   11°C

–9°C   –8°C   –3°C   –5°C   –12°C   0°C

Test 14 Days in the months

Work out the following sums by adding together the days in the given months. Write your answers in the spaces and check them with the number-spotter.

*Thirty days has September, April, June and November
All the rest have thirty-one, excepting February alone,
And that has twenty-eight days clear, and twenty-nine in each leap year.*

July and March ———

January and September ———

May and August ———

December and June ———

February (not leap year) and April ———

April, May and June ———

July, August and September ———

November, December and January ———

October, March and leap year February ———

Test 15 Sequences

Look at each of the following sequences to see how they work. Then add the missing numbers. Check your answers with the number-spotter.

145   147   149   151   ___   ___   ___

28   37   46   55   ___   ___   ___

68   61   54   47   ___   ___   ___

348   345   342   339   ___   ___   ___

___   ___   75   79   ___   87   91   ___

222   ___   210   ___   198   ___   186   180

125   ___   ___   200   ___   250   275

Test 16 Multiples

Circle the correct answers in each list. Check your answers with the number-spotter.

Circle each number that is a multiple of…

2	71 298 409 550 823
5	26 75 104 360 663
4	12 20 34 46 53
3	9 16 18 25 30
10	45 80 153 372 530

Circle each number that will <u>not</u> divide equally by…

2	14 27 65 89 100
5	31 50 66 75 90
10	60 143 290 401 670
3	13 18 25 27 30
4	8 11 19 23 32

Test 17 Fractions

Write the following amounts in the spaces. Then check your answers with the number-spotter. The first one has been done for you.

$\frac{1}{4}$ of 16   _____4_____

$\frac{1}{2}$ of 30   _____

$\frac{1}{3}$ of 21   _____

$\frac{1}{10}$ of 70   _____

$\frac{1}{5}$ of 25   _____

$\frac{1}{4}$ of 100   _____

$\frac{1}{2}$ of £1   _____

$\frac{1}{4}$ of 1m   _____

$\frac{1}{10}$ of £1   _____

$\frac{1}{10}$ of 1m   _____

$\frac{1}{5}$ of £1   _____

$\frac{1}{2}$ of 1m   _____

$\frac{1}{2}$ of 1kg   _____

$\frac{1}{10}$ of 1km   _____

$\frac{1}{4}$ of 1kg   _____

$\frac{1}{5}$ of 1km   _____

Test 18 Money

Rewrite the following amounts as instructed. Then check your answers with the number-spotter. Some of them have been done for you.

Write in pence…

£1.36 — 136p

£6.85 — _____

£12.10 — _____

£25.04 — _____

£5.77 — _____

£10.05 — _____

Write in pounds…

267p — £2.67

841p — _____

1520p — _____

3073p — _____

6033p — _____

123p — _____

Test 19 Addition and subtraction

Complete the following questions. Write your answers in the spaces. Then check your answers with the number-spotter.

454 add 50 = _____

73 take away 8 = _____

total 36 and 29 = _____

increase 38 by 32 = _____

take 7 from 82 = _____

53 subtract 26 = _____

decrease 63 by 35 = _____

41 plus 120 = _____

add 17 to 93 = _____

270 less 150 = _____

22 less than 146 = _____

40 more than 79 = _____

111 plus 1000 = _____

subtract 130 from 225 = _____

total 8, 19 and 5 = _____

280 minus 96 = _____

take 55 from 312 = _____

999 take away 101 = _____

203 more than 98 = _____

add 75 to 463 = _____

Test 20 Doubles and halves

Complete the following questions. Write your answers in the spaces. Then check your answers with the number-spotter.

26 + 26 = _____

double 42 = _____

half of 76 = _____

twice 35 = _____

90 + 90 = _____

460 divided by 2 = _____

double 210 = _____

twice 380 = _____

5000 divided by 2 = _____

1500 + 1500 = _____

twice 490 = _____

half of 2400 = _____

700 + 700 = _____

double 270 = _____

half of 5200 = _____

twice 800 = _____

290 + 290 = _____

half of 3800 = _____

double 180 = _____

2600 divided by 2 = _____

Test 21 Remainders

Complete the following questions by writing the missing part of each sum in the space provided. Then check your answers with your number-spotter.

43 = 10 x 4 + __3__

68 = 6 x 10 + __8__

34 = 5 x 6 + __4__

16 = 3 x 5 + __1__

23 = 4 x 5 + __3__

29 = 9 x 3 + __7__

44 ÷ 5 = 8 remainder __4__

32 ÷ 10 = 3 remainder __2__

37 ÷ 3 = 12 remainder __1__

22 ÷ 4 = 5 remainder __2__

6 x 10 + __7__ = 67

7 x 5 + __4__ = 39

8 x 3 + __2__ = 26

4 x 4 + __1__ = 17

Test 22 Angles

Estimate the angles below. Write your estimates in the spaces. Then check with your number-spotter to see how close you were.

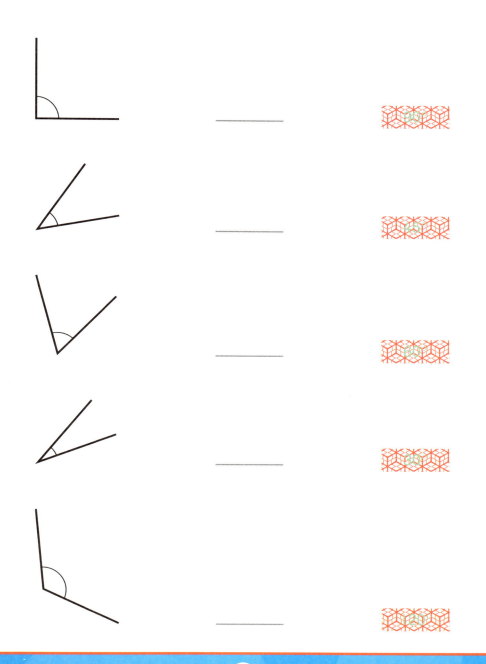

Test 23 Adding 3 numbers

Complete the following questions. Write your answers in the spaces. Then check your answers with the number-spotter.

81 + 38 + 20 = ____

17 + 43 + 35 = ____

27 + 52 + ____ = 110

32 + 63 + ____ = 145

70 + ____ + 36 = 127

44 + ____ + 75 = 172

____ + 97 + 63 = 204

____ + 73 + 51 = 225

112 + 65 + ____ = 245

124 + ____ + 43 = 278

____ + 81 + 150 = 250

69 + 104 + ____ = 265

45 + 122 + ____ = 270

____ + 92 + 105 = 289

135 + ____ + 72 = 310

119 + 84 + ____ = 325

Test 24 How long?

Complete the following questions. Write your answers in the spaces. Then check your answers with the number-spotter.

A film lasts 2 hours 10 minutes.

It started at 7.22pm.

What time does it finish? _____

The match started at 2pm.

The teams played 45 minutes each way.

The half-time break was 10 minutes.

When did the match finish? _____

John got up at 7.40am.

He left home 50 minutes later.

He arrived at school at 8.45am.

How long did his journey to school take? _____

Jenny's train journey back from town took 1 hour 40 minutes.

The walk home from the station took 10 minutes.

She arrived home at 9.12pm.

What time did the train leave town? _____

Mike has tennis practice every other Tuesday.

He last went on 9th June.

What date will it be the next time he goes? _____

Test 25 Multiplication and division

Complete the following questions. Write your answers in the spaces. Then check your answers with the number-spotter.

10 x 7 = 70

50 ÷ 5 = 10

15 x 6 = 90

28 ÷ 4 = 7

45 ÷ 9 = 5

32 ÷ 2 = 16

8 x 6 = 48

11 x 3 = 33

75 ÷ 3 = 25

36 ÷ 3 = 12

3 x 23 = 69

21 x 3 = 63

20 x 5 = 100

44 ÷ 4 = 11

120 ÷ 12 = 10

8 x 20 = 160

Test 26 Money problems

Complete the following questions. Write your answers in the spaces. Then check your answers with the number-spotter.

One book costs £2.99.

How much for 3 books? _____

4 packs of sausages cost £3.64.

How much for 1 pack? _____

A comic costs 65p.

How many can you buy for £2? _____

How much change do you get? _____

I buy 3 boxes of chocolates at £4.26 each.

How much did I pay? _____

What was my change from £20? _____

I have £10. I bought 5 bottles of squash.

My change was £2.10.

How much was each bottle of squash? _____

My train fare is £3.40.

I must put the correct change in the ticket machine.

I have 2 x £1, 3 x 50p, 1 x 20p and 3 x 10p.

Which coins will I have left? _____

Test 27 Which sign?

Make each of the following sums read correctly by adding the correct function sign. Check your answers with the number-spotter. The first one has been done for you.

29 __+__ 31 = 60

27 _____ 3 = 9

82 _____ 29 = 53

15 _____ 2 = 30

32 _____ 2 = 16

40 _____ 6 = 240

53 _____ 17 = 70

64 _____ 20 = 44

7 _____ 20 = 140

77 _____ 7 = 11

25 _____ 5 = 5

71 _____ 36 = 107

95 _____ 76 = 19

12 _____ 5 = 60

63 _____ 7 = 9

105 _____ 25 = 80

Test 28 Perimeters

A perimeter is the distance around the edge of any shape. Estimate the perimeters of the shapes below in centimetres. Write your estimates in the spaces. Then check them with the number-spotter.

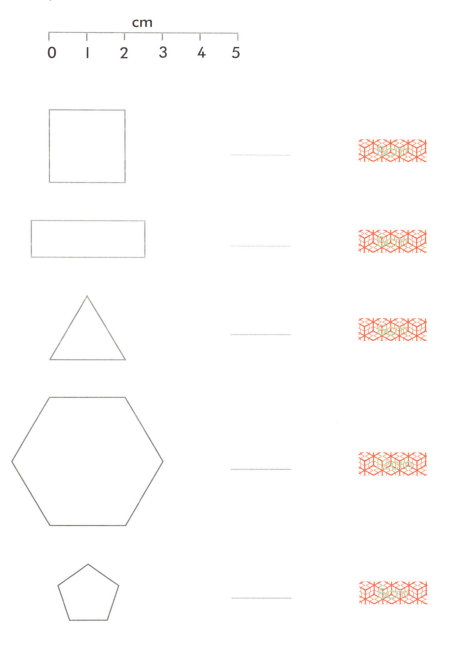

Test 29 Measuring problems

Read the following problems and answer the questions. Write your answers in the spaces. Then check them with your number-spotter.

A bottle of medicine holds 200 millilitres.

How many 5ml spoons are in the bottle? _____

A bag of sweets weighs 240g.

How much would 10 bags weigh? _____

It is 435 miles to Grandma's.

We stop for lunch after 219 miles.

How much further is there still to travel? _____

A full jug holds 2 litres.

A full glass holds $\frac{1}{3}$ of a litre.

How many glasses will the jug fill? _____

Two planks are 64cm and 92cm long.

They were cut from a larger plank 2m long.

How much wood is left? _____

A 4km race is run over 16 laps.

How long is each lap? _____

After 10 laps how much of the race is left? _____

Test 30 Mixed bag

Complete the following questions. Write your answers in the spaces. Then check them with your number-spotter.

90	+	_____	=	130
349	+	3	=	_____
200	÷	50	=	_____
400	−	7	=	_____
40	x	_____	=	400
192	−	25	=	_____
300	+	473	=	_____
386	+	_____	=	400
500	÷	_____	=	50
25	x	8	=	_____
804	−	789	=	_____
64	÷	_____	=	8
12	x	20	=	_____
1742	−	4	=	_____
4100	+	_____	=	5000
2000	÷	10	=	_____
30	x	20	=	_____
609	−	21	=	_____
252	+	49	=	_____
400	÷	5	=	_____

Keep your score!

	Score 1st time	2nd time		Score 1st time	2nd time
Test 1			Test 16		
Test 2			Test 17		
Test 3			Test 18		
Test 4			Test 19		
Test 5			Test 20		
Test 6			Test 21		
Test 7			Test 22		
Test 8			Test 23		
Test 9			Test 24		
Test 10			Test 25		
Test 11			Test 26		
Test 12			Test 27		
Test 13			Test 28		
Test 14			Test 29		
Test 15			Test 30		